EXTREME PREDATORS

BLACKBIRCH PRESS

An imprint of Thomson Gale, a part of The Thomson Corporation

THOMSON

★

GALE

Detroit • New York • San Francisco • San Diego • New Haven, Conn. • Waterville, Maine • London • Munich

THOMSON

GALE

For more information, contact
Blackbirch Press
27500 Drake Rd.
Farmington Hills, MI 48331-3535
Or you can visit our Internet site at http://www.gale.com

Photo credits: Cover: top center, top right Corel Corporation; top left © PhotoDisc; bottom right © Photos.com; bottom left © Digital Vision; middle right © Digital Stock; middle left © Eyewire/PhotoDisc/Getty Images; all pages © Discovery Communications, Inc., except for pages 1, 20 © PhotoDisc; page 4 © Digital Vision; page 8 © Stephen Dalton/Photo Researchers, Inc.; pages 12, 16, 32 Corel Corporation; page 24 © Ken Lucas/Visuals Unlimited; page 28 © Digital Stock; page 30 Department of Defense/Petty Officer 3rd Class Jeffrey S. Viano, U.S. Navy; page 34 (large) © Reuters/CORBIS; page 36 © Eyewire/PhotoDisc/Getty Images; page 40 © Photos.com

LIBRARY OF CONGRESS CATALOGING-IN-PUBLICATION DATA

Predators / John Woodward, book editor.
    p. cm. — (Planet's most extreme)
Includes bibliographical references and index.
   ISBN 1-4103-0396-9 (hardcover : alk. paper) — ISBN 1-4103-0438-8 (paper cover : alk. paper)
  1. Predatory animals—Juvenile literature. 2. Psychology, Comparative—Juvenile literature. I. Woodward, John, 1958–. II. Series.

  QL758.P733 2005
  591.5'3—dc22
                                           2004018321

Printed in the United States of America
10 9 8 7 6 5 4 3 2 1

Just when you thought it was safe to get back in the water, along come the scariest killers in the natural world. We're counting down the top ten most extreme predators in the animal kingdom and seeing what happens when hunters become the hunted. Discover that there's always time to kill when predation is taken to The Most Extreme.

The **Crocodile**

Hiding at number ten in the countdown is the crocodile. It's easy to see why the crocodile is an extreme predator. These cold-blooded killers can be three times longer and ten times heavier than the average man!

But it takes more than just great size and strength to become number ten in the countdown. Crocodiles may only have a brain the size of your thumb, but they're smart predators.

Hiding in the water and waiting for your lunch to arrive may seem like a simple hunting technique, but crocodiles have turned it into an art form. They can spend up to a month watching and waiting, learning what's happening in their killing ground.

With its eyes and nose just above the water, a crocodile does its famous impersonation of a floating log. But when it's time to close in for the kill, it disappears.

Doesn't the crocodile at the top look like a floating log? The water buffalo (bottom) sure thought so, and he's paying dearly for his mistake.

Scientists believe that crocs feel their way forward, tiptoeing slowly towards their prey. Crocodiles learn the contours of the bottom and can read it like a map.

Jennifer Butler (right) teaches a client that the best way to survive the urban jungle of Los Angeles is to shop for bargains.

Just like crocodiles, humans have had to hunt to survive for thousands of years. Today, some human predators hunt for different prey. Jennifer Butler doesn't hunt for food, but for bargains. She is a professional shopper in Los Angeles, California. This makes her sort of an urban predator.

In today's world of supermarkets and restaurants, most humans no longer have to kill to survive. Butler uses all the hunting skills of her ancient ancestors to help clients track down items in the urban jungle. She describes the most important trait of a successful hunter:

> *The most important skill is focus. A hunter needs focus to find the item. In most hunters it might be the animal they're looking for. For me, it's the object that I'm looking for that represents the person most effectively at the greatest value. I need to know the stores, from the discount to the great designer stores. And I need to know what my clients' needs are.*

Sitting in the sun all day, crocodiles really don't need a lot of energy. One big meal is enough to keep them going for an entire year.

Like crocodiles, urban predators learn their hunting grounds and patiently search out the perfect target before making a killing. The only difference is that when crocodiles make a purchase, there's usually no refund.

Crocodiles don't have to hunt very often. They really are cold-blooded killers, which means a half-ton croc sitting in the sun all day uses the same amount of energy as a sparrow! A big croc can survive a whole year on just one big dinner. Our other contenders have to kill much more frequently, which is why the mighty crocodile is only number ten in the countdown.

7

The **Archerfish**

Once upon a time in Sherwood Forest, there lived a hunter who preyed on the rich. He was Robin Hood, perhaps the most famous archer of all time. Only one animal could rival Robin Hood: the archerfish.

It lives under the trees of a very different forest in Southeast Asia. Here, there are so many fish down in the mangrove roots that sometimes food can be hard to find. But the archerfish has worked out a truly extreme way to get it.

The archerfish knocks its food into the water by spitting. It's number nine in the countdown because it can squirt a jet of water more than eight times its own body length. That's like an average man spitting over 40 feet! It's better than the best baseball player at calculating where its plummeting prey will splash down. It needs only one-tenth of a second to judge the catch, which is very important when there are other hungry mouths waiting in the outfield.

Spotting a bug on a mangrove leaf, an archerfish uses its extreme jet of water to knock it off.

With aim that would make an archerfish jealous, Lee Wheelis spits watermelon seeds into a jar from far away.

Even the archerfish would be jealous of Lee Wheelis from Luling, Texas. With just one slice of watermelon, Wheelis can become a human archerfish. He describes his special skill:

My wife and I were at the competition, and she said, "Are you going to try your luck again this year?" And I said, "Yeah, I'll go try to spit the seed again." The first seed didn't hardly leave my mouth, and she hollered at me and said, "You've got to do better than that." So I put the seed in my mouth and reared back and let it fly. Then everyone in the audience started getting excited. It had gone past the previous record to a distance of 68 feet, 9 inches. Being from Texas, I don't like to brag, but I could probably spit a watermelon seed through a keyhole at 30 paces.

The secret to his success is in the way he rolls his tongue, and an awful lot of practice. Imagine the damage an archerfish could cause if it could spit like Lee Wheelis. Perhaps it's lucky that watermelons don't grow in the mangrove swamps of Southeast Asia.

It's a good thing the archerfish doesn't have to compete with Wheelis. He's just launched a seed all the way across his driveway.

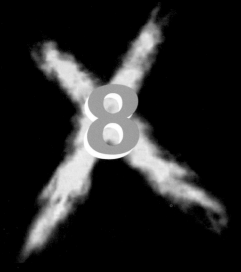

8

The **Polar Bear**

The frozen wasteland of the Arctic is home to number eight in our countdown of extreme predators. The polar bear is one awesome killing machine.

An adult polar bear can weigh as much as seven men. One swipe of its huge paw could take out prey three times its size! But the polar bear's nose is by far its most important weapon, for in this barren wasteland finding something to kill can be difficult. A polar bear can sniff out a seal over twenty miles away, using a sense of smell 100 times better than ours. No wonder some people call them "noses with legs."

It's even thought that a polar bear can detect a seal hiding beneath three feet of ice. Locating the seal is one thing. Breaking though the ice is another.

Polar bears are only successful in about 10 percent of their attacks on hidden seals. Perhaps they would have more luck if they adopted some of the latest technology available to human hunters.

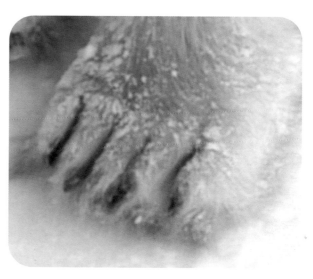

Locating a seal hiding beneath the ice, a polar bear gets ready to use its massive paws to break through the surface.

13

Law enforcement officers now have a device that allows them to search buildings from the outside. It lets them see through concrete walls!

The motion detector radar works by projecting energy beams through solid concrete. The frequency of the radar signal is unaffected by stone, but bounces back off the water in a living body. By studying the reflected signals, it's possible for the police to determine the location and movement of suspects inside the building.

Motion-detecting radar (top) gives people the power of X-ray vision. Using radar (middle), officers spot a suspect hiding behind a wall (bottom).

14

Fed up with trying to catch seals, this polar bear is grazing on small plants growing among the rocks.

A polar bear would kill for a motion detector radar, because in this frozen land, food is hard to find, and even harder to catch. Sometimes a polar bear can go for weeks without making a kill, so it's no wonder that in summer this mighty predator finds a different dietary supplement! Because it sometimes eats plants, which are easier to catch, the polar bear is only number eight in the countdown.

7

The Spider

The next contender in our countdown of extreme predators is the ultimate creepy crawly. It doesn't take much imagination to see why the spider is number seven in the countdown. There are more than 35,000 different spiders in the world. All of them are predators that use one of the most remarkable hunting devices in the animal kingdom. Weight for weight, the silk in a spider's web can be five times as strong as steel, twice as elastic as nylon, and can hold 4,000 times its own weight.

To turn silk into a trap, an orb web spider releases a single thread into the wind. When the free end catches hold, the spider cinches up the silk and attaches the thread to the web's starting point. From this bridge the spider lays down the basic support structure for the web, before finishing it off with a spiral of the sticky silk used to trap its prey.

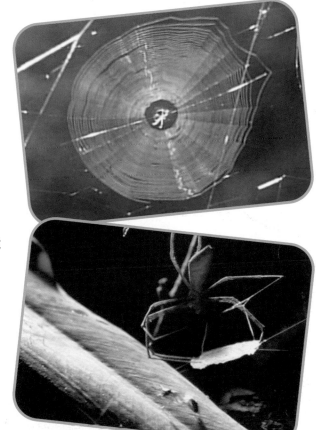

One extreme spider prefers to knit a portable web. It's easy to see how the net-casting spider gets its name. But spiders aren't the only ones to use nets for catching their prey. Some humans have copied the net-casting spider in the fight against crime.

Spider web silk sure makes a deadly trap. With a bug in sight, a net-casting spider spins a small web and wraps up her dinner to go.

17

For U.S. law enforcement officers, there's a new way of bringing back criminals alive. Inside a cartridge fired from a standard tear-gas launcher is a device that would make Spider-Man proud.

The Webshot Capture Net fires a Kevlar mesh net up to 30 feet and is designed to control people carrying weapons other than firearms. The aim is to bring down the suspect safely and to minimize the risks for the arresting officer.

Spider-Man would love the Webshot Capture Net. One shot from an officer's cannon, and the bad guy is tangled in its trap.

If you travel to South America, you can find another way to use a web to safely bring down a target from a distance. The bola is a weapon made by fastening two stone balls on either end of a cord of rawhide. When Patagonian Indians throw it, the bola twists around the legs of the animal, bringing it down.

One animal has been hunting with a bola for a lot longer than humans. In Australia, the female magnificent spider uses a bola to catch male moths. Her bola is scented with pheromones to make it smell like a female moth. This is one spider that really has lunch on the fly.

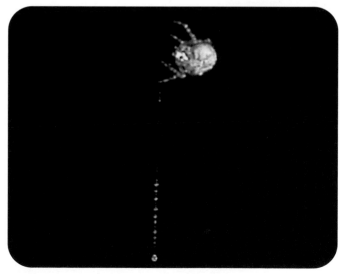

A Patagonian Indian shows how easy the bola is to use (top). This magnificent spider (bottom) uses her own type of bola to attract moths to eat.

19

6 The Snake

Don't bother hiding from the next contender. It can track you down even on the darkest night. The snake slides into number six in the countdown because it's a predator with highly sophisticated sensory equipment. It can taste the air with its tongue, and its unblinking eyes detect the smallest movements.

You can run, but you can't hide! Using infrared sensors that detect body heat, this snake easily tracks down a tasty rat.

This snake also has infrared sensors tucked into the pits along its lips that let it "see" wavelengths of light that humans only feel as heat. These infrared sensors feed their information to the same part of the brain as the eyes do. That means the snake has the heat sensor's thermal image superimposed over the visual image of its prey. It's a deadly combination.

21

People, however, need technology to turn night into day. Thanks to thermal imaging cameras, humans can now see like snakes. The heat generated by a living body stands out from the cooler, darker surroundings. That's why law enforcement agencies around the world have installed thermal imaging cameras on helicopters. Now suspects can't hide under the cover of darkness. As any snake knows, there are huge advantages for hunters if they can see in the dark.

Heat-seeking technology is one thing, but now it's possible to detect the presence of cold steel. We've all seen scanners at airports search for concealed weapons. Now scientists are developing a portable radar unit that can detect a weapon's unique specific electromagnetic

Thermal imaging cameras on helicopters (top) help police find bad guys in the dark. A monitor (bottom) shows officers where suspects are hiding.

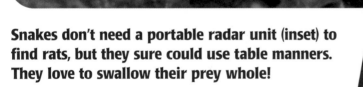

Snakes don't need a portable radar unit (inset) to find rats, but they sure could use table manners. They love to swallow their prey whole!

resonance. The aim is to make a portable scanner for law enforcement officers to detect concealed weapons from a distance, making arrests much safer for both officers and suspects.

A snake may not be able to detect a criminal's concealed weapon, but a rat can't hide from it. When a snake eats a rat whole, the massive mouthful will take many minutes to swallow and many days to digest. This is why, despite their deadly reputation, snakes don't kill very often, unlike the next contenders in the countdown.

23

The Electric Eel

There's something fishy about the next extreme predator. Visitors to the Amazon are terrified of the stories of deadly piranha–fish that can strip your flesh to the bone in seconds. But there's a predator in these waters that's much scarier than piranha. It's even scarier than the caiman crocodile. The most frightening predator in these waterways has no teeth at all, but a truly shocking secret. Meet the electric eel.

This caiman gets the shock of its life as an electric eel uses its high-voltage tail to zap every part of the croc's body.

Each electric shock from an electric eel is generated from up to 200,000 linked electrochemical cells that make up about four-fifths of the eel's tail. They combine to pack a punch five times stronger than what you get if you stick your finger in a power socket! It's more than enough power to stun a caiman.

The electric eel is number five in the countdown because of the way it uses electricity. Low-voltage pulses are used to navigate and locate fish. The eel's high voltages are simply stunning. It's an extreme way of hunting, so it's no wonder that electricity is used to catch both fish and criminals.

Law enforcement is now using electricity to stop criminals. Police often use the Taser, which is an electric shock device, to deliver 50,000 volts of electricity into a suspect's body. This stuns the criminal so he or she can be arrested. This is often preferable to using firearms because it usually doesn't kill the suspect.

Before using the Taser (top) on criminals, these officers stun each other with the device so they know just how strong the shock is.

If this electric eel were a police officer, he sure wouldn't need a Taser gun to stun criminals. He could just turn his tail on them!

Many police officers go through a training program to learn what it's like to get hit by a Taser. They take turns getting stunned themselves so they have a better understanding of how powerful the Taser is. Getting hit by an electric eel would be just as shocking.

The Shark

There is another fish that can turn a pleasant swim in the water into a nightmare: the shark. The great white shark strikes from below. Powered by two tons of muscle, it can make a simple change of direction to cut off all escape routes.

With razor-sharp teeth and excellent vision, hearing, and smell, the shark is a deadly predator. The seal above is easy prey for a great white.

Those massive jaws and razor-sharp teeth are infamous, but they're not much use if you can't find your prey in the big blue sea. That's why sharks are armed with very sophisticated senses.

These extreme predators have excellent eyes, ears, and noses, and they can even detect tiny electrical signals from their prey. It's no surprise that when the U.S. military came up with the flying equivalent of the shark, they called it the "Predator."

This small, unmanned reconnaissance aircraft can be used to spy on enemy positions, sending data back to a base over 460 miles away. As machines like the Predator grow more and more sophisticated, our bodies are starting to get in the way. That's why scientists at the Wright-Patterson Air Force Base in Ohio are trying to connect the mind directly to the machine. Brain-actuated control systems mean that you can move the cockpit of a flight simulator simply by thinking about turning. It's hoped that one day this system will be installed in fighter planes so that pilots can attack at the speed of thought!

The Predator (below) helps the U.S. military to keep an eye on enemies, while simulators teach pilots to become one with their aircraft (right).

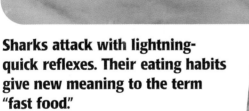

Sharks attack with lightning-quick reflexes. Their eating habits give new meaning to the term "fast food."

Shark attacks also happen at great speed. It's just that they don't happen very often. Despite their bad reputation, sharks can go for weeks without making a kill, which is why they're only number four in the countdown.

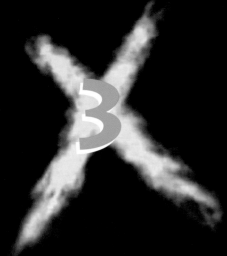

3

The **Wolf**

The next contender can run twice as fast as an Olympic sprinter and is strong enough to bring down animals more than eight times its own weight. The reason the wolf is number three in the countdown is because these killers work as a team. Once the pack has singled out a victim, they run it down, using their numbers to attack from all sides. When it comes to hunting as a team, the wolf is the leader of the pack.

Wolves hunt in a pack (top). Once the pack manages to take down prey, the wolves really wolf down their food.

Hunting together lets the pack bring down bigger animals than a single wolf could hope to kill on its own. Even so, it's estimated that only one out of ten attacks is successful. That's why wolves really know how to wolf down their food. In a single meal, one wolf can swallow the equivalent of 88 hamburgers!

The wolf pack is such an efficient hunting unit that it's no wonder it inspired a different group of hunters. In the past, Native Americans saw wolves as teachers. They sought to emulate the way wolf families worked together.

It was inspiration from another fighting animal, however, that gave rise to a new nation in Africa at the end of the 18th century. Shaka, king of the Zulu empire, used a revolutionary new fighting tactic based on the most important animal in the tribe, the bull.

In the 18th century, the Zulu people of Africa adopted a war strategy inspired by the tribe's most important animal, the bull.

When approaching an enemy position, Shaka would first send out the horns—the fastest warriors—to surround the enemy. Then in went the chest—the veteran fighters leading the frontal attack. The loins were kept in reserve and sent in to secure the kill. Working together as a team has obvious benefits for both humans and wolves.

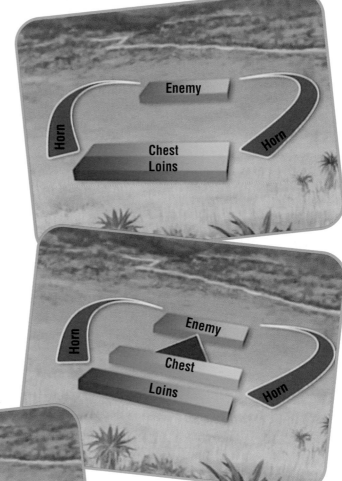

The bull strategy of King Shaka looked like this: First, he sent warriors to surround the enemy (top); next, fighters attacked the front (middle); finally, fighters in reserve finished the job.

35

2

The Orca

The wolf pack is an extremely effective hunting unit, killing at least once a week. But it's no match for the next contender. There's another pack of extreme predators that have been called the "wolves of the sea." Number two in the countdown eats sharks for breakfast! The ancient Romans called it orca orcinus. It is orca, the killer whale.

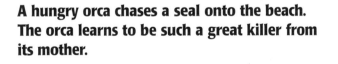

**A hungry orca chases a seal onto the beach.
The orca learns to be such a great killer from
its mother.**

It's hard to comprehend just how big and how
strong the killer whale really is. Try to imagine an animal the size of
an elephant that can swim six times faster than an Olympic swim-
mer! A pod of orcas work like a wolf pack and can basically kill
anything in the sea, from stingrays to great white sharks.

Orcas have one of the biggest brains in the animal kingdom, but
they are not natural born killers. A mother must train her calf to
become a predator.

Real-life private detective Tom Barnes admits that he spends far more time at his desk than he does chasing his prey.

Despite their ferocious reputation, there are no records of killer whales ever attacking a human. To catch a human requires a very different set of skills. Just ask any private detective.

Thanks to the movies, many people think that those who track humans for a living spend their days dodging bullets in fast cars. But for the 39,000 private investigators in America, the reality is very different.

Los Angeles–based private investigator Tom Barnes knows that locating humans that don't want to be found means spending more time in front of a computer than behind the wheel of a fast car.

As with any predatory animal, finding his prey is half the detective's battle. That's where modern technology makes the job much easier. Global positioning systems make it relatively simple to track a suspect from afar. Barnes can enhance his hearing with parabolic microphones, his eyes with thermal imaging devices, and his memory with the most commonly used tool in the trade—the camcorder.

Being a private investigator may look easy, but don't be fooled. To successfully make a catch in this business requires more than just patience. He explains:

> Being a good private investigator is like being a good fisherman. You've got to know where to fish, when to fish, what kind of bait to use, and when to reel them in.

Barnes makes use of technology like a global positioning system (top) and a camcorder to make him a more efficient predator.

The Shrew

Nothing can beat the orca when it comes to catching fish, but even this massive predator can't compete with an animal that has to kill every two hours or die. The most extreme predator in the countdown is the shrew. Shrews are not human killers, but they really are extreme predators. No other animal has to kill so often.

The shrew eats constantly to fuel its speedy metabolism. By contrast, the elephant (inset, background) takes its time to chew because its metabolism is so slow.

Shrews may be the smallest mammals on Earth, but they have a massive appetite. Armed with poisonous saliva, they can paralyze prey even if it's twenty times their size! A keen sense of smell and a bunch of whiskers help them find their way to the kill.

Shrews are constantly hunting because they have to consume at least their own body weight in food each day to fuel their incredibly fast metabolism. The heart of a shrew beats nine times faster than a human's. That's an incredible 600 times a minute as the shrew races around looking for food! In comparison, an elephant's heart beats only 25 times a minute.

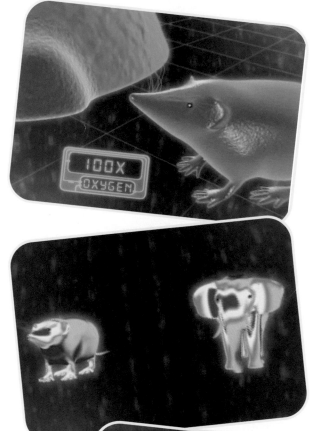

Given the shrew's frantic lifestyle, it's no surprise that it needs vast amounts of energy to survive. Weight for weight, a shrew burns through 100 times more oxygen than an elephant! A lot of energy goes into just staying warm. If a shrew died it would cool down in minutes, because it quickly loses heat over its surface area. A dead elephant, however, might take days to cool down. If a shrew had the slow metabolic rate of an elephant, it would need fur nearly a yard thick to keep warm!

The shrew needs lots of oxygen (top) to keep warm, while the elephant gets by with much less (middle). If the shrew had an elephant's metabolism, it would need very thick fur (bottom)!

To eat three times our weight every day like the shrew, we'd have to stuff our faces with nearly 2,000 burgers (inset)!

The shrew doesn't have a lot of fur. Instead, it has a big appetite to fuel its extraordinary metabolism. One kind of shrew has to eat up to three times its own weight in food every 24 hours. To keep pace, an adult human would have to eat 1,920 hamburgers each day!

43

Unfortunately, in America today some people are eating like they have the shrew's metabolism. According to the American Heart Association, more than 30 percent of adults are clinically obese.

Part of the problem seems to be that Americans have lost their predatory lifestyle. Once humans had to burn off body fat hunting their food. Now the only exercise some people get is walking around the supermarket!

Because it's so easy to stock up on food at the grocery store, many Americans eat like they have the metabolism of a shrew.

Blink twice and the shrew, The Most Extreme predator, will be off again in search of its next meal.

Life would be so much easier for shrews if they could visit a supermarket. Instead, the only way the shrew can get all the calories it needs to survive is to be the busiest hunter in the world. Don't let its tiny size fool you. For when it comes to hunting, the shrew really is The Most Extreme.

For More Information

Mary M. Cerullo, *The Truth About Great White Sharks.* San Francisco: Chronicle, 2000.

Kathleen W. Deady, *Great White Sharks, Vol. 1*. Mankato, MN: Capstone, 2001.

Eleanor J. Hall, *Polar Bears*. San Diego: KidHaven Press, 2002.

Alice B. McGinty, *Jumping Spider.* New York: Rosen, 2003.

Darlyne Murawski, *Spiders and Their Webs.* Washington, DC: National Geographic Society, 2004.

Amanda O'Neill, *I Wonder Why Snakes Shed Their Skin and Other Questions About Reptiles.* New York: Houghton Mifflin, 2003.

Jason Stone and Jody Stone, *Polar Bear.* San Diego: Blackbirch Press, 2001.

Lily Wood and Carolyn Otto, *Wolves.* New York: Scholastic, 2001.

Glossary

bola: a weapon consisting of a cord with weights at each end

brain-actuated: to move an object by thought

global positioning system: a satellite-based system for locating things

metabolism: all the chemical processes in a living organism

obese: grossly overweight

parabolic microphone: a device that allows the user to hear distant sounds

pheromones: chemicals produced by animals that stimulate or attract other animals

poisonous: injurious or lethal to an organism

predator: animal that hunts other animals for food

reconnaissance: preliminary military survey

thermal imaging device: a device that can identify things by the heat they radiate, even in the dark

Index